BRIDGES

MAN-MADE WONDERS

Jason Cooper

Rourke Enterprises, Inc.
Vero Beach, Florida 32964

PHOTO CREDITS

© Lynn M. Stone: title page, pages 4, 10, 13, 15, 17, 18, 21;
© James P. Rowan: cover, page 7; © Jerry Hennen: pages 8, 12

LIBRARY OF CONGRESS
Library of Congress Cataloging-in-Publication Data
Cooper, Jason, 1942-
  Bridges / by Jason Cooper.
  p.   cm. — (Man made wonders)
  Includes index.
  Summary: Discusses the history and uses of bridges and
cites several famous examples.
  ISBN 0-86592-628-X
  1. Bridges—Juvenile literature.   [1. Bridges.]
I. Title.   II. Series.
TG148.C66   1991
624'.2—dc20   91-11532
                                         CIP
                                         AC

TABLE OF CONTENTS

BRIDGES

Bridges make travel easier. Where nature does not provide a passage, a bridge can. Bridges are platforms that reach over waterways and other difficult crossings.

Most bridges are built for cars, trucks, and trains. A few bridges have been built at airports to allow airplanes to rumble over highways.

People who are walking use footbridges to cross streams and busy streets.

Many bridges of great length or special design have become well known.

Railroad trestle bridge over the
Flathead River in Montana

FAMOUS BRIDGES

Perhaps no bridge is better known than the first London Bridge. It was built of stone in London, England, in 1176.

California's Golden Gate Bridge (1937) is one of America's most famous bridges. The Golden Gate rises over San Francisco Bay.

Florida's dazzling Sunshine Skyway (1987) takes cars and trucks over Tampa Bay. The Seven Mile Bridge in the Florida Keys is known for its remarkable length.

The famous Brooklyn Bridge (1893) in New York was designed by John A. Roebling, the "father" of suspension bridges.

The new Tower Bridge at night in London, England

EARLY BRIDGES

The first bridges may have been tree trunks that fell across streams. The first planned bridges that we know about were built about 4,000 years ago.

Early bridges were built of stone, brick, and wood. Bridges continued to be built from these materials until the first iron bridges were made about 200 years ago. By the late 1800s, steel and concrete were used in most bridges.

Many styles of bridges have been built. The biggest modern bridges use steel lines called **cables** for support.

An old arch bridge built of stone

BRIDGE BUILDING

The building of a major bridge is a huge job. First, supports for the bridge must be built into solid ground, often under water. Above these supports are others, which meet the bridge itself.

Tall, steel towers may rise from the bridge roadway. Cables are attached to the towers. They help support the bridge. The roadway for cars and trucks is one of the last parts to be built.

Cables, towers, piers support the Golden Gate Bridge over San Francisco Bay, California

Steel cables help suspend the Dewey Bridge over the Colorado River near Moab, Utah

Two-span bridge over the Connecticut River at East Haddam, Connecticut

COVERED BRIDGES

Covered bridges were once common in America, especially in the New England states. Covered bridges were made of wood. They looked like long, open-ended barns. The platform itself was the floor. It was protected by walls and a peaked roof.

The roof and walls kept rain and snow from soaking and rotting the bridge floor.

In the early 1900s, cars and trucks replaced horses. The narrow covered bridges, built for horses, could not handle cars and trucks very well. Many covered bridges were torn down. The remaining covered bridges are rare.

Covered bridge in Grafton, Vermont

DRAWBRIDGES

Long ago, castles were surrounded by a ditch filled with water. A drawbridge over the ditch, known as a moat, let people leave the castle and cross the moat. When the bridge was not in use, it could be raised—drawn upward.

Today's drawbridges are driven by motors. They serve ships, not castles. They lift so that large boats may pass safely underneath.

Drawbridge rises for a passing boat in Sarasota, Florida

SUSPENSION BRIDGES

The most graceful bridges and the biggest ones are suspension bridges. Some of the world's most famous bridges are of this type.

Suspension bridges use thousands of feet of cables. Each cable is a line of tightly wrapped steel wires.

In suspension bridges, the cables are anchored to solid ground. Then they are attached from one bridge tower to the next.

The cables hold up, or **suspend,** the roadway of the bridge.

Bay Bridge, a suspension bridge between Oakland and San Francisco, California

MORE SUSPENSION BRIDGES

Some suspension bridges rise 700 feet above water. The largest main **span** on a suspension bridge is 4,600 feet, nearly one mile. The main span is the distance between bridge towers.

Cable-stayed bridges are not as large as that, but they are also bridges with cables and towers.

Unlike suspension bridges, modern cable-stayed bridges have cables directly from their towers to the bridge deck.

Florida's Sunshine Skyway, a modern, cable-stayed bridge

OTHER KINDS OF BRIDGES

Architects have designed many kinds of bridges. One of the most common is the beam bridge. Beam bridges are simple and fairly short. They are often used on new highways.

Long beam bridges have supports underneath them. The supports may be posts or a framework of wood or steel known as a trestle. Trestle also refers to almost any railroad bridge.

Glossary

architect (ARK uh tekt) — someone who designs buildings, bridges

cable (KAY bul) — a strong steel rope

span (SPAN) — an arch over something, or the distance between two points of support on a bridge

suspend (sus PEND) — to hold up in such a way as to be free on all sides except at the points of support

INDEX